The Darkest

Serial Killers

with Their Stories

Coloring Book For Adults

Born: December 24, 1939
Fort Wayne, Indiana, U.S

Number of Victims: 28

Died: August 8, 1973
Pasadena, Texas, U.S.

Cause of death : Gunshot wounds to left chest and back

Nickname : *The Candy Man*

Dean Arnold Corl was an American serial killer who abducted, raped, tortured, and murdered at least 28 teenage boys and young men between 1970 and 1973 in Houston, Texas. He was aided by two teenaged accomplices, David Owen Brooks and Elmer Wayne Henley. The crimes, which became known as the Houston Mass Murders, came to light after Henley fatally shot Corll. Upon discovery, it was considered the worst example of serial murder in U.S. history.

Corll's victims were typically lured with an offer of a party or a lift to a succession of addresses in which he resided between 1970 and 1973. They would then be restrained either by force or deception, and each was killed either by strangulation or shooting with a .22 caliber pistol. Corl and his accomplices buried 17 of their victims in a rented boat shed; four other victims were buried in woodland near Lake Sam Rayburn; one victim was buried on a beach in Jefferson County; and at least six victims were buried on a beach on the Bolivar Peninsula. Brooks and Henley confessed to assisting Corl in several abductions and murders; both were sentenced to life imprisonment at their subsequent trials.

Corll was also known as the Candy Man and the Pied Piper, because he and his family had previously owned and operated a candy factory in Houston Heights, and he had been known to give free candy to local children

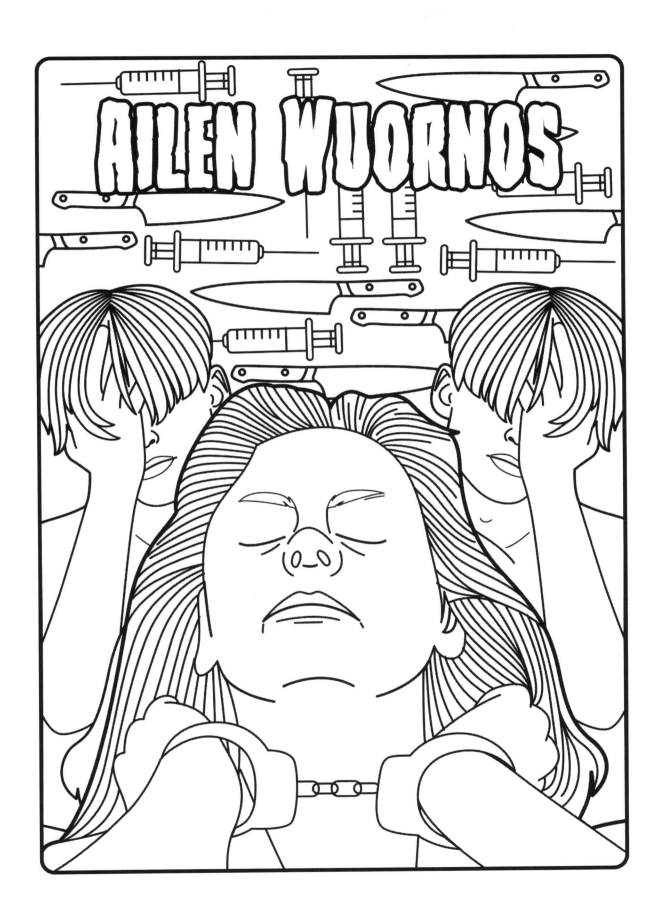

Born: February 29, 1956
Rochester, Michigan, United
States

Number of Victims: 7

Died: October 9, 2002 (aged
46) Florida State Prison,
Bradford County, Florida,
United States

Cause of death : Execution by
lethal injection

Nickname : _Damsel of Death_

Aileen Carol "Lee" Wuornos was an American serial killer
and prostitute who murdered seven men in Florida in 1989
and 1990 by shooting them at point-blank range. Wuornos
claimed that her victims had either raped or attempted to
rape her while she was servicing them, and that all of the
homicides were committed in self-defense. She was
sentenced to death for six of the murders and was executed
by lethal injection on October 9, 2002.

The 2003 film Monster chronicles Wuornos' story from
childhood until her first murder conviction. It stars Charlize
Theron as Wuornos, a performance that earned Theron an
Academy Award for Best Actress

Born: **November** 24, 1946
Burlington, Vermont, U.S.

Number of Victims:30
confessed; total unconfirmed

Died: January 24, 1989
Florida State Prison, Bradford
County, Florida, United States

Cause of death : Execution byelectrocution

Nickname : *The campus killer*

Theodore Robert Bundy was an American serial killer who kidnapped, raped, and murdered numerous young women and girls during the 1970s and possibly earlier. After more than a decade of denials, before his execution in 1989 he confessed to 30 homicides that he committed in seven states between 1974 and 1978. The true number of victims is unknown and possibly higher.

Bundy was regarded as handsome and charismatic, traits that he exploited to win the trust of victims and society. He would typically approach his victims in public places,feigning injury or disability, or impersonating an authority figure, before knocking them unconscious and taking them to secluded locations to rape and strangle them. He sometimes revisited his secondary crime scenes, grooming and performing sexual acts with the decomposing corpses until putrefaction and destruction by wild animals made any further interactions impossible. He decapitated at least 12 victims and kept some of the severed heads as mementos in his apartment. On a few occasions, he broke into dwellings at night and bludgeoned his victims as they slept.

In 1975, Bundy was jailed for the first time when he was incarcerated in Utah for aggravated kidnapping and attempted criminal assault. He then became a suspect in a progressively longer list of unsolved homicides in several states. Facing murder chargesin Colorado, he engineered two dramatic escapes and committed further assaults in Florida, including three murders, before his ultimate recapture in 1978. For the Florida homicides, he received three death sentences in two trials. Bundy was executed in the electric chair at Florida State Prison in Raiford, Florida on January 24, 1989.

Born: May 19, 1870
Washington, D.C., U.S.

Number of Victims: 3 confirmed
9–100+ possible/claimed

Died: January 16, 1936 Sing
Sing Correctional Facility,
Ossining, New York, U.S.

Cause of death : Executed
by electric chair

Nickname : _The Gray Man_

Hamilton Howard "Albert" Fish was an American serial killer, child rapist and cannibal. He was also known as the Gray Man, the Werewolf of Wysteria, the Brooklyn Vampire, the Moon Maniac, and The Boogey Man. Fish once boasted that he "had children in every state", and at one time stated his number of victims was about 100. However, it is not known whether he was referring to rapes or cannibalization, nor is it known if the statement was truthful.

Fish was a suspect in at least five murders during his lifetime. He confessed to three murders that police were able to trace to a known homicide, and he confessed to stabbing at least two other people. Fish was apprehended on December 13, 1934, and put on trial for the kidnapping and murder of Grace Budd. He was convicted and executed by electric chair on January 16, 1936, at the age of 65. His crimes were dramatized in the 2007 film The Gray Man, starring Patrick Bauchau as Fish.

Born: 25 October 1879
Hanover, German Empire

Number of Victims :
24-27+

Died: 15 April 1925
Hanover, Weimar Republic

Cause of death : Decapitation
by guillotine

Nickname : _the Butcher of Hanover_

Friedrich Heinrich Karl "Fritz" Haarmann (25 October 1879 – 15 April 1925) was a German serial killer, known as the Butcher of Hanover, the Vampire of Hanover and the Wolf-Man, who committed the sexual assault, murder, mutilation and dismemberment of at least 24 boys and young men between 1918 and 1924 in Hanover, Germany.

Haarmann was found guilty of 24 of the 27 murders for which he was tried and sentenced to death by beheading in December 1924. In addition, in accordance with German practice, his honorary rights of citizenship were revoked. He was subsequently executed in April 1925.

Haarmann became known as the Butcher of Hanover (German: Der Schlächter von Hannover) due to the extensive mutilation and dismemberment committed upon his victims' bodies and by such titles as the Vampire of Hanover (der Vampir von Hannover) and the Wolf-Man (Wolfsmensch) because of his preferred murder method of biting into or through his victims' throats

Born: April 17, 1946
Orlando, **Florida**, **United States**

Number of Victims : 20-35+

Died: December 18, 1974
Georgia, United States

Cause of death :Gunshot wound

Nickname : *The Casanova Killer*

Paul John Knowles (April 17, 1946 – December 18, 1974), also known as The Casanova Killer, was an American serial killer tied to the deaths of 20 people in 1974, though he claimed to have taken 35 lives.

Born in Orlando, Florida, his father gave him up to live in foster homes and reformatories after he was convicted of a petty crime. Knowles himself was first incarcerated at the age of 19, and in the years following, he spent more time in prison.

Knowles' cross-country murder spree began in Jacksonville on the night of his escape. He broke into the home of 65-year-old Alice Curtis, bound and gagged her, ransacked her home for money and valuables, then stole her car. Curtis choked to death on her gag.

On the street where he intended to abandon the car, Knowles recognized family acquaintances Lillian and Mylette Anderson. Lillian was eleven years old and her sister Mylette was seven. In fear that they would identify him, he kidnapped them both, strangled them, and buried their bodies in a nearby swamp.

Knowles was finally cornered on November 17 by 27-year-old former Vietnam War Veteran and hospital maintenance worker David Clark

Born:24 July 1909
Stamford, Lincolnshire,
England

Number of Victims: 6-9

Died:10 August 1949
Wandsworth Prison,
Wandsworth, London,
England

Cause of death :Execution by
hanging

Nickname : the Acid Bath
Murderer

John George Haigh, commonly known as the Acid Bath Murderer, was an English serial killer who was convicted for the murders of six people, although he claimed to have killed nine. Haigh battered to death or shot his victims and disposed of their bodies using sulphuric acid before forging their signatures so he could sell their possessions and collect large sums of money.

Born: March 9, 1945 (age 75)
Pittsburg, Kansas, U.S.

Number of Victims:10

Nickname :*The BTK Killer*

Dennis Lynn Rader (born March 9, 1945) is an American serial killer known as BTK (an abbreviation he gave himself, for "bind, torture, kill") or the BTK Strangler. Between 1974 and 1991, Rader killed ten people in Wichita and Park City, Kansas, and sent taunting letters to police and newspapers describing the details of his crimes.After a decade-long hiatus, Rader resumed sending letters in 2004, leading to his 2005 arrest and subsequent guilty plea. He is serving ten consecutive life sentences at El Dorado Correctional Facility in Prospect Township, Butler County, Kansas.

Born: Charles Chi-tat Ng
24 **December** 1960 (**a**ge 59)
British Hong Kong

Number of Victims: 11-25+

Charles Chi-tat Ng is a convicted Hong Kong-American serial killer who committed numerous crimes in the United States. He is believed to have raped, tortured and murdered between 11 and 25 victims with his accomplice Leonard Lake at Lake's cabin in Calaveras County, California, in the Sierra Nevada foothills, 60 miles from Sacramento. After his 1985 arrest and imprisonment in Canada on robbery and weapons charges,
followed by a lengthy dispute between Canada and the US, Ng was extradited to California, tried, and convicted of 11 murders.He is currently on death row at San Quentin State Prison.

Born: May 21, 1960

Milwaukee, Wisconsin, U.S.

Died: November 28, 1994

Columbia, Wisconsin, U.S.

Cause of death :Homicide (severe head trauma)

Nickname :_The Milwaukee Cannibal_

Number of Victims: 17

Jeffrey Lionel Dahmer, also known as the Milwaukee Cannibal or the Milwaukee Monster,
was an American serial killer and sex offender who committed the murder and dismemberment of 17 men and boys from 1978 to 1991. Many of his later murders
involved necrophilia, cannibalism, and the permanent preservation of body parts—typically all or part of the skeleton.

Although he was diagnosed with borderline personality disorder, schizotypal personality disorder, and a psychotic disorder, Dahmer was found to be legally sane at his trial. He
was convicted of 15 of the 16 murders he had committed in Wisconsin, and was sentenced to 15 terms of life imprisonment on February 15, 1992.Dahmer was later sentenced to a 16th term of life imprisonment for an additional homicide committed in Ohio in 1978.

Dahmer served his time at the Columbia Correctional Institution in Portage, Wisconsin.
During his time in prison, Dahmer expressed remorse for his actions and wished for his own death. He also read the Bible and declared himself a born-again Christian, ready for his final judgment. He was attacked twice by fellow inmates, with the first attempt to slice his neck open leaving him with only superficial wounds. However, he was attacked a second time on November 28, 1994, by an inmate as they cleaned one of the prison showers. Dahmer was found still alive, but died on the way to the hospital from severe head trauma.

Born: May 12, 1897
San Francisco, **California**, U.S.
Died: January 13, 1928
Winnipeg, Manitoba, Canada
Cause of death : Execution by hanging
Nickname : *Gorilla man*

Number of Victims: 22+

Earle Leonard Nelson, also known in the media as the "Gorilla Man," the "Gorilla Killer," and the "Dark Strangler," was an American serial killer, rapist, and necrophile. He was the first known American serial sex murderer of the twentieth century. Born and raised in San Francisco, California by his devoutly Pentecostal grandmother, Nelson exhibited bizarre behavior as a child, which was compounded by head injuries he sustained in a bicycling accident at age ten. After committing various minor offenses in early adulthood, he was institutionalized in Napa for a time.

Nelson began committing numerous rapes and murders in February 1926, primarily in the West Coast cities of San Francisco and Portland, Oregon. In late 1926, he moved east, committing multiple rapes and murders in several Midwestern and East Coast cities, before moving north into Canada, raping and killing a teenage girl in Winnipeg, Manitoba. After committing his second murder in Winnipeg, he was arrested by Canadian authorities and convicted of both murders, and sentenced to death. Nelson was executed by hanging in Winnipeg in 1928.

In undertaking his crimes, Nelson had a modus operandi: Most of his victims were middle-aged landladies, many of whom he would find through "room for rent" advertisements. Posing as a mild-mannered and charming Christian drifter, Nelson used the pretext of renting a room in the landladies' boardinghouses to make contact with them before attacking. Each of his victims were killed via strangulation, and many were raped after death. His penultimate victim, a 14-year-old girl named Lola Cowan, was the only known victim to be significantly mutilated after death.

Nelson's crime spree, which consists of 22 known murders, made him the most prolific serial killer by convictions in American history until the discovery of Juan Corona's crimes in 1971, and was a source of inspiration for Alfred Hitchcock's 1943 film Shadow of a Doub

Born:14 January 1946

Number of Victims: 215+

Nottingham, **Nottinghamshire**, England

Died:13 January 2004 (aged 57)

HM Prison Wakefield,England

Cause of death :Suicide by hanging

Nickname : Dr death

Harold Frederick Shipman known to acquaintances as Fred Shipman, was an English general practitioner who is believed to be the most prolific serial killer in modern history.

On 31 January 2000, Shipman was found guilty of the murder of 15 patients under his care; his total number of victims was approximately 250. Shipman was sentenced to life imprisonment with the recommendation that he never be released. He committed suicide by hanging on 13 January 2004, a day before his 58th birthday, in his cell at Wakefield Prison.

The Shipman Inquiry, was a two-year-long investigation of all deaths certified by Shipman,
which Dame Janet Smith chaired, examined Shipman's crimes. The inquiry identified 215 victims and estimated his total victim count at 250, about 80 percent of whom were elderly women. Shipman's youngest confirmed victim was a 41-year-old man, although suspicion arose that he had killed patients as young as four.He is the only British doctor known to be guilty of murdering his patients, although other doctors have been acquitted of similar crimes or convicted on lesser charges

Born: April 18, 1947 (age 73)
Salinas, **California**, U.S.

Number of Victims: 13

Nickname :_The Psychopath of Santa Cruz_

Herbert William Mullin (born April 18, 1947) is an American serial killer who killed thirteen people in California in the early 1970s. He confessed to the killings, which he claimed prevented earthquakes. He noted that there were no earthquakes during his killing spree, and felt vindicated when a Mw 5.8 earthquake hit the area soon after his arrest.[citation needed] In 1973, after a trial to determine whether he was insane or culpable, he was convicted of two murders in the first degree and nine in the second, and sentenced to life imprisonment. He has been denied parole 10 times and is unlikely to ever be released

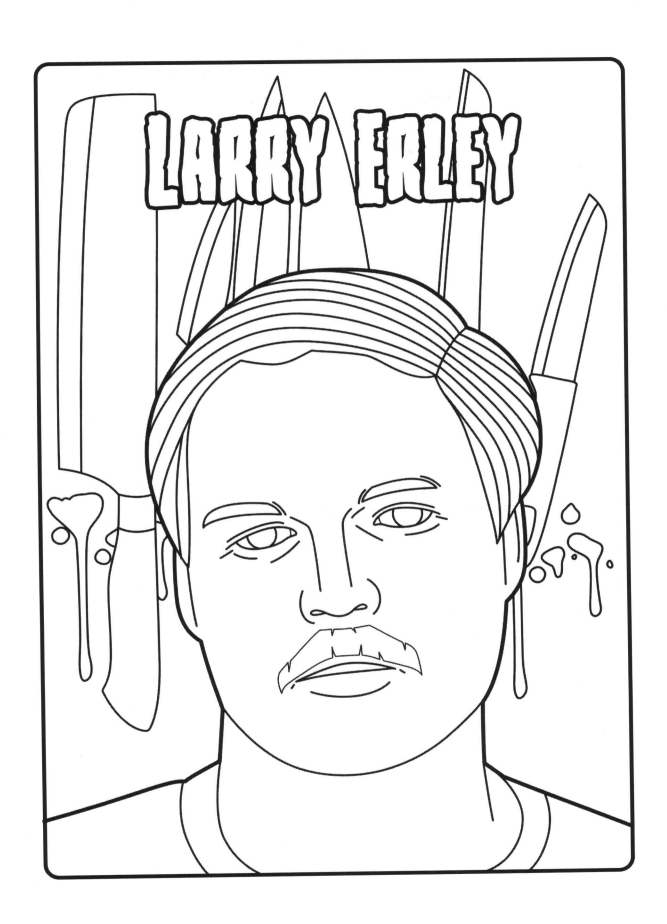

Born: December 21, 1952
 Indiana, U.S.

Died: March 6, 1994 (aged 41)
Pontiac, Illinois, U.S.

Cause of death :AIDS-related
complications

Number of Victims:
21-24

Nickname :_The interstate killer_

Larry William Eyler was an American serial killer who is believed to have murdered a minimum of twenty-one teenage boys and young men in a series of killings committed between 1982 and 1984 in the Midwestern States. Convicted and sentenced to death by lethal injection for the 1984 kidnapping and murder of 16-year-old Daniel Bridges,
Eyler later voluntarily confessed to the 1982 murder of 23-year-old Steven Ray Agan,
offering to also confess to his culpability in twenty further unsolved homicides if the state of Illinois would commute his sentence to one of life imprisonment without parole.

Eyler died of AIDS-related complications in 1994 while incarcerated on death row.
Shortly before his death, he confessed to the murders of twenty further young men and boys to his defense attorney, Kathleen Zellner, although he denied being physically responsible for the actual murder of Daniel Bridges, which he insisted had been committed by an alleged accomplice in five of his homicides, Robert David Little.

With her client's consent, Zellner posthumously released Eyler's confession following the formal announcement of his death.

Eyler was known as the "Interstate Killer" and the "Highway Killer" due to the fact many of his confirmed and alleged victims were discovered across several Midwestern States in locations close to or accessible via the Interstate Highway System

Born:25 January 1957 (age 63)

Génova, **Quindío**, **Colombia**

Nickname : _La Bestia_

Number of Victims: 138 confirmed 300 claimed

Luis Alfredo Garavito Cubillon also known as La Bestia ("The Beast") or Tribilín (named after the Disney character "Goofy") is a Colombian
rapist and serial killer. In 1999, he admitted to the rape, torture and murder of 138 boys and teenagers. His victims, based on the locations of skeletons listed on maps that Garavito drew in prison, could exceed 300; Garavito continues to confess to more murders. He has been described by local media as "the world's worst serial killer." The Guinness Book of World Records lists another Colombian, Pedro Alonso López, known in Colombia as "the Monster of the Andes," as
the largest-scale serial killer of modern times; however, in terms of the number of confirmed victims Garavito tops the list followed by López. The judicial body ruled that all Garavito's sentences total 1,853 years and nine days in jail.
Garavito's victims were clearly identified by their age, gender, and social status. Garavito targeted boys between the ages of 6 to 16 who were either homeless, peasants, or orphaned. He would approach the young boys, either on the crowded streets or alone in the countryside, and lure them away by bribing them with small gifts such as money, candy or odd jobs. He offered easy work for money and even disguised himself as different characters who could be seen as legitimately offering work to the boy, such as a priest, a farmer, a homeless man, a street vendor, a drug dealer, an elderly man, and a gambler. The bodies of the children were all found completely naked, and all bore bite marks. Most corpses showed signs of prolonged torture

Born: December 26, 1950 (age 69) Salem, Oregon, U.S.

Number of Victims: 18-41

Nickname : *The I-5 Killer*

Randall Brent "Randy" Woodfield is an American serial killer, rapist, kidnapper, and robber who was dubbed the I-5 Killer or the I-5 Bandit by the media due to the crimes he committed along the Interstate 5 corridor running through Washington, Oregon, and California. Before his capture, the I-5 Killer was suspected of multiple sexual assaults and murders. Though convicted in only one murder, he has been linked to a total of 18, and is suspected of having killed up to 44 people.

A native of Oregon, Woodfield was the third child of a prominent Newport family. He began to exhibit abnormal behaviors during his teenage years, and was arrested for indecent exposure while still in high school. An athlete for much of his life, Woodfield played as a wide receiver for the Portland State Vikings, and was drafted by the NFL in 1974 to play for the Green Bay Packers, but was cut from the team during training after a series of indecent exposure arrests.

In 1975, Woodfield began a string of robberies and sexual assaults on women in Portland, which he committed at knifepoint. Between 1980 and 1981, he committed multiple murders in cities along the I-5 corridor in Washington, Oregon, and California; his earliest-documented murder was that of Cherie Ayers, a former classmate whom he had known since childhood, in December 1980. After committing numerous robberies, sexual assaults, and murders, Woodfield was arrested in March 1981, and convicted in June of the murder of Shari Hull and attempted murder of her co-worker, Beth Wilmot, and sentenced to life imprisonment plus 90 years. In a subsequent trial, he was convicted of sodomy and improper use of a weapon in a sexual assault case, receiving 35 additional years to his sentence.

Woodfield has never confessed to any of the crimes of which he has been accused or convicted. Though he has only been convicted of one murder and one attempted murder, he has been linked via DNA and other methods to numerous unsolved homicides in the ensuing decades. Authorities have estimated his total number of killings to be as many as 44, and CBS News named him one of the deadliest serial killers in American history.He is currently incarcerated at the Oregon State Penitentiary.

Born:February 29, 1960
El Paso, Texas, U.S.
Nickname :T*he night stalker*

Number of Victims: 14

Ricardo Leyva Muñoz Ramírez , known as Richard Ramirez, was an American serial killer,
serial rapist, and burglar. His highly publicized home invasion crime spree terrorized the residents of the greater Los Angeles area and later the residents of the San Francisco area from June 1984 until August 1985. Prior to his capture, Ramirez was dubbed the "Night Stalker" by the news media.

He used a wide variety of weapons, including handguns, knives, a machete, a tire iron, and a hammer. Ramirez, who claimed to be a Satanist, never expressed any remorse for his crimes. The judge who upheld Ramirez's nineteen death sentences remarked that his deeds exhibited "cruelty, callousness, and viciousness beyond any human understanding".Ramirez died of complications from B-cell lymphoma while awaiting execution on California's death row.
Psychiatrist Michael H. Stone describes Ramirez as a 'made' psychopath as opposed to a 'born' psychopath. He says that Ramirez's schizoid personality disorder contributed to his indifference to the suffering of his victims and his untreatability

Born:May 16, 1861
Gilmanton, U.S
Died:May 7, 1896 (aged 34)
Cause of death : Execution

Number of Victims:
20 to 200

Nickname : _The beast of chicago_

Herman Webster Mudgett , better known as Dr. Henry Howard Holmes or H. H. Holmes,
was an American serial killer. While he confessed to 27 murders,he was convicted and sentenced to death for only one murder, that of accomplice and business partner Benjamin Pitezel. Despite his confession of 27 murders after the Pitezel trial awaiting execution, it is speculated that Holmes may have killed as many as 200 people.Victims were killed in a mixed-use
building which he owned, located about 3 miles (5 km) west of the 1893 World's Fair: Columbian Exposition, supposedly called the World's Fair Hotel (informally called "The Murder Castle"), though evidence suggests the hotel portion was never truly open for business.

Besides being a serial killer, Holmes was also a con artist and a trigamist, the subject of more than 50 lawsuits in Chicago alone. Holmes was executed on May 7, 1896, nine days before his 35th birthday

Born: May 23, 1950
Sacramento, California, U.S.
Died: December 26, 1980 (aged
30) San Quentin State Prison,
California, U.S
Cause of death :Suicide by
overdose

Number of Victims:6

Nickname :*The Vampire of
Sacramento*

Richard Trenton Chase was an American serial killer, rapist, cannibal, and necrophile
who killed six people in the span of a month in Sacramento, California. He was
nicknamed "The Vampire of Sacramento" because he drank his victims' blood and
cannibalized their remains.
On December 29, 1977, Chase killed his first known victim in a drive-by shooting. The
victim, Ambrose Griffin, was a 51-year-old engineer and father of two.

On January 23, 1978, Chase broke into a house and shot Teresa Wallin (three months
pregnant at the time) three times. He then had sexual intercourse with her corpse
while stabbing her with a butcher knife. He then removed multiple organs, cut off one
of her nipples and drank her blood. He stuffed dog feces from Wallin's yard down her
throat before leaving.
On January 27, Chase entered the home of 38-year-old Evelyn Miroth. He
encountered her friend, Danny Meredith, whom he shot with his .22 handgun, then
took Meredith's wallet and car keys. He then fatally shot Miroth, her six-year-old son
Jason, and her 22-month-old nephew David Ferreira, before mutilating Miroth and
engaging in necrophilia and cannibalism with her corpse.

Born:February 15, 1939
Estherville, Iowa, U.S.
Died:August 21, 2014 (aged 75)
Anchorage, Alaska, U.S.
Cause of death : Natural
causes

Number of Victims:17–21

Nickname : _The Butcher Baker_

Robert Christian Hansen known in the media as the "Butcher Baker," was an American serial killer. Between 1971 and 1983, Hansen abducted, raped, and murdered at least 17 women in and around Anchorage, Alaska; he hunted many of them down in the wilderness with a Ruger Mini-14 and a knife. He was arrested and convicted in 1983, and was sentenced to 461 years and a life sentence without the possibility of parole.

Robert Hansen was born in Estherville, Iowa, in 1939. He was the son of a Danish immigrant and followed in his father's footsteps as a baker. In his youth, he was skinny and painfully shy, afflicted with a stutter and severe acne that left him permanently scarred. Shunned by the attractive girls in school, he grew up hating them and nursing fantasies of cruel revenge

Born: 9 April 1974 (age 46)
Mytishchi, **M**oscow **O**blast,
Russian SFSR, USSR
Nickname : _The chess board killer_

Number of Victims: 48-60

Alexander Yuryevich Pichushkin born 9 April 1974), also known as The Chessboard Killer and The Bitsa Park Maniac , is a Russian serial killer. He is believed to have killed at least 48 people, and possibly as many as 60, between 1992 and 2006 in Southwest Moscow's Bitsa Park, where a number of the victims' bodies were found. In 2007 he was sentenced to life imprisonment.

Pichushkin is remembered to have been an initially sociable child. However, this changed following an incident in which Pichushkin fell backwards off a swing, which then struck him in the forehead as it swung back. Experts speculated that this event damaged the frontal cortex of Pichushkin's brain; such damage is known to produce poor impulse regulation and a tendency towards aggression. Since Pichushkin was still a child, the damage would have been more severe, as a child's forehead provides only a fraction of the protection for the brain than an adult's. Following this accident, Pichushkin frequently became hostile and impulsive

Russian media has speculated that Pichushkin was motivated, in part, by a macabre competition with another notorious Russian serial killer, Andrei Chikatilo, the 'Rostov Ripper', who was convicted in 1992 of killing 53 children and young women over a 12-year period.Pichushkin has said his aim was to kill 64 people, the number of squares on a chessboard. He later recanted this statement, saying that he would have continued killing indefinitely had he not been stopped

TIAGO GOMES DA ROCHA

Born:4 February 1988 (age 32) Goiânia, Brazil

Number of Victims: 39

Nickname : _The motorbike killer_

Tiago Henrique Gomes da Rocha is a Brazilian former security guard and serial killer who has claimed to have killed 39 people. He approached his victims on a motorbike and shouted "robbery" before shooting them. However, he never took anything.He targeted homeless people, women and homosexuals in Goiás. His youngest victim was a 14-year-old girl killed in January 2014 and 16 of his victims were women. Gomes da Rocha was arrested after being caught riding a motorbike with a fake plate. He earlier caught the attention of police after they discovered that he was facing trial for stealing the number plate off a motorbike at a supermarket in Goiania in January 2014. A motorbike, stolen plates and the suspected murder weapon, a .38 revolver, were retrieved from a home he shared with his mother. He attempted suicide in his prison cell on 16 October 2014 by slashing his wrists with a smashed light bulb.Gomes da Rocha has claimed to have gained murderous urges after being sexually abused by his neighbor at age 11.

In May 2016 he was convicted of eleven murders and sentenced to 25 years in prison.

Born:Andrei Romanovich Chikatilo
16 **O**ctober 1936
Died:14 February 1994 (aged 57)Novocherkassk, Rostov Oblast, Russia
Cause of death :Execution by shooting
Nickname : _The Red Ripper_

Number of Victims:52-56+

Andrei Romanovich Chikatilo 16 October 1936 – 14 February 1994) was a Soviet serial killer, nicknamed the Butcher of Rostov, the Red Ripper, and the Rostov Ripper, who sexually assaulted, murdered, and mutilated at least 52 women and children between 1978 and 1990 in the Russian SFSR, the Ukrainian SSR, and the Uzbek SSR. Chikatilo confessed to 56 murders and was tried for 53 of these killings in April 1992. He was convicted and sentenced to death for 52 of these murders in October 1992, although the Supreme Court of Russia ruled in 1993 that insufficient evidence existed to prove Chikatilo's guilt in nine of these murders. Chikatilo was subsequently executed in February 1994.

Chikatilo was known as the "Rostov Ripper" and the "Butcher of Rostov" because he committed most of his murders in the Rostov Oblast of the Russian SFSR.

Born: January 8, 1947

Willimantic, **Connecticut**, U.S.

Died: February 23, 1996 (aged 49) San Quentin State Prison, San Quentin, California, U.S.

Cause of death :Execution by lethal injection

Nickname : The freeway killer

Number of Victims:14-31

William George Bonin , also known as the Freeway Killer, was an American serial killer
and twice-paroled sex offender who committed the rape, torture, and murder of a minimum of 21 boys and young men in a series of killings in 1979 and 1980 in southern California.
Bonin is also suspected of committing a further 15 murders. Described by the prosecutor
at his first trial as "the most arch-evil person who ever existed",Bonin was convicted of 14 of the murders linked to the "Freeway Killer" in two separate trials in 1982 and 1983. He spent 14 years on death row before he was executed by lethal injection at San Quentin State Prison in 1996.

Bonin became known as the "Freeway Killer" due to the fact that the majority of his victims'
bodies were discovered alongside numerous freeways in southern California. He shares this epithet with two separate and unrelated serial killers: Patrick Kearney and Randy
Kraft.

Born:June 28, 1964

Oakland, **California**, U.S.

Died: April 3, 2014 (aged 49)

Huntsville, Texas, U.S.

Cause of death :Lethal injection

Nickname :*The Cross-country Killer*

Tommy Lynn Sells (June 28, 1964 – April 3, 2014) was an American serial killer. He was convicted of one murder, for which he received the death penalty and was eventually executed. Authorities believe he committed a total of 22 murders.
Sells and his twin sister, Tammy Jean, contracted meningitis when they were 18 months old; Tammy died from the illness. Shortly thereafter, Sells was sent to live with his aunt, Bonnie Walpole, in Holcomb, Missouri. When he was five years old, he was returned to his mother after she found out his aunt wanted to adopt him.

Sells claimed that when he was eight, he began spending time with a man named Willis Clark, who began to molest him with the consent of his mother. Sells stated that this abuse affected him greatly, and he would relive his experiences while committing his crimes.

The homeless Sells hitchhiked and train-hopped across the United States from 1978 to 1999, committing various crimes along the way. He held several very short-term manual-labor and barber jobs. He drank heavily, abused drugs, and was imprisoned several times

Number of Victims:22+

Printed in Great Britain
by Amazon